Searching for Love

In All the Wrong Places

A Journey from Rejection to Restoration, Finding *True Love* in the One Who Never Fails.

God's love leads you to the *right place.*

DR. TONJA ALEXANDER

Searching For Love In All The Wrong Places

Dr. Tonja Alexander

ISBN: 979-8-9962875-2-9

Published by
ACT Publishing
An imprint of A Caring Touch Design & Publishing

Dedication to God

To My Heavenly Father,

This book is lovingly dedicated to You.

Thank You for loving me before I knew how to love myself.

Thank You for seeing me when I felt invisible, holding me when I felt broken, and pursuing me when I was searching for love in all the wrong places.

When I was looking for acceptance, You called me Your daughter.

When I was searching for my worth, You reminded me that I was fearfully and wonderfully made.

When I was wounded, You became my Healer.

When I felt abandoned, You proved that You would never leave me nor forsake me.

Thank You for Your grace that covered my mistakes, Your mercy that gave me another chance, and Your unconditional love that transformed my life.

Thank You for taking the broken pieces of my story and creating a testimony that points others to You.

Every chapter of this book is a reminder that true love is not found in people, possessions, or positions, it is found in You.

You are the Perfect Father.

You are my Protector.

You are my Provider.

You are my Peace.

You are my Redeemer.

You are the One who taught me what genuine love looks like.

My prayer is that every person who reads these pages will encounter Your presence, experience Your healing, and discover the immeasurable depth of Your love.

May every wounded daughter find her identity in You.

May every father be inspired to reflect Your heart.

May every family experience restoration.

May every life be transformed by Your truth.

All glory, all honor, and all praise belong to You.

Thank You for allowing me to tell my story so that others may discover Yours.

With all my love, gratitude, and worship,

Your Daughter,

Dr. Pastor Tonja Alexander
"We love because He first loved us."
— 1 John 4:19

Dedication to My Mentor

To My Mentor, Dr. Bishop Leroy Davis,

With sincere gratitude and deep respect, I dedicate this book to you.

Thank you for believing in me, challenging me, and encouraging me to grow beyond what I thought was possible. Your wisdom, leadership, and unwavering commitment to the Gospel have helped shape not only my ministry but also my understanding of God's heart for families.

Thank you for teaching me the profound importance of a father's presence in his daughter's life during the foundational years of birth through twelve years of age. That revelation has forever changed the way I view healing, identity, and God's divine design for the family. It became one of the driving forces behind this book.

Thank you for pushing me to the next level under your leadership. You saw gifts in me that I had not yet fully recognized in myself, and you continually challenged me to walk boldly in the calling God placed on my life.

Thank you for trusting me with the responsibility of spreading the Gospel of Jesus Christ. Your confidence in me inspired me to serve with greater faith, greater purpose, and greater humility.

Your mentorship has been a blessing, your leadership an example, and your investment in my life a gift that I will always treasure.

May God continue to strengthen you, enlarge your territory, and bless the work of your hands as you continue to impact lives for His Kingdom.

With heartfelt appreciation and honor,

Dr. Pastor Tonja Alexander

TABLE OF CONTENTS

My Truth

Don't judge me.

I never claimed to be perfect.

I simply chose to tell the truth about my journey.

You know my story because I had the courage to share it.

I don't know yours because you haven't told it.

We all have a past.

We all have scars.

We all have moments we wish we could rewrite.

The difference is that I chose to let God use my brokenness as a testimony of His grace.

So don't judge my story.

Instead, let it remind you that if God could heal me, restore me, forgive me, and give me purpose, He can do the same for you.

My past is not my identity.

God's grace is.

Chapter 1

The First Man in Her Life

Why Fathers Matter from Birth Through Twelve

"The righteous man walks in his integrity; his children are blessed after him." — Proverbs 20:7 (NKJV)

Every daughter has a story about the first man she ever loved—her father.

Whether he was present every day, absent altogether, or somewhere in between, his influence leaves fingerprints on her heart. Before she ever understands romance, she is learning about love. Before she ever enters a relationship, she is discovering what protection feels like. Before she ever hears another man call her beautiful, she has already formed beliefs about her value.

From birth through the age of twelve, a father helps shape a daughter's identity. During these formative years, she learns trust, security, confidence, boundaries, and self, worth. A father's words can become the voice she hears long after she becomes an adult. His presence or his absence—can influence how she views herself, how she relates to others, and even how she understands God as her Heavenly Father.

Notice I said *presence,* not simply *proximity*. A father can live in the same home and still be emotionally unavailable. He can provide financially and still leave a daughter longing to be seen. Presence is more than occupying space. Presence is giving your heart, your attention, your encouragement, your guidance, and your love.

My Reflection: My Daddy

The first man in my life was my father and he truly lived up to his name.

My parents divorced when I was around four years old. Although I spent a lot of time at my father's house, he wasn't truly present. As a little girl, however, none of that mattered to me. I believed my daddy was the strongest man in the world. In my eyes, nobody could beat him.

One memory has stayed with me all these years.

My mother had to take me to the emergency room because I needed a shot. I was terrified. I screamed, cried, kicked, and fought with everything I had because I didn't want that needle.

In the middle of all the chaos, I shouted, "My daddy is going to beat you up!"

A little while later, my father walked into the room. I immediately jumped into his arms and begged him to beat up the doctor because he had given me the shot.

To a frightened little girl, my father represented strength and protection. I believed he could fix anything.

As I grew older, however, I began to realize there was a difference between someone being around and someone being present.

My father was often physically there, but emotionally, spiritually, and relationally, there were moments when I needed more than his presence in the room, I needed his presence in my life.

That realization became one of the greatest lessons of my childhood.

A father's greatest gift is not simply showing up. It is making his daughter feel seen, heard, protected, valued, and deeply loved.

Today, I understand that fathers are human. They have wounds, disappointments, and struggles of their own. Some simply love the best way they know how because no one showed them differently.

This chapter is not about assigning blame. It is about recognizing influence.

The first man in a daughter's life helps write the first chapters of her understanding of love. Those chapters may not determine the ending of her story, but they often explain how the story begins.

The beautiful news of the Gospel is that where earthly fathers fall short, our Heavenly Father never does. He sees every tear, heals every wound, and restores every broken place. Through Christ, no daughter has to remain defined by what she lacked. She can be transformed by the perfect love of the Father who has never abandoned her.

Reflection Questions

1. What is one of your earliest memories of your father or the father figure in your life?
2. Did you experience your father as present, absent, or somewhere in between?
3. What messages did you receive about your worth as a little girl?
4. How have those early experiences influenced your adult relationships?
5. In what areas do you need God to rewrite your understanding of love?

Scripture Study

Read: Psalm 68:5-6

Key Truth: God identifies Himself as "a Father to the fatherless." He steps into the places where earthly fathers may have been absent or unable to provide what we needed.

Additional Scriptures for Meditation:

- Proverbs 22:6
- Ephesians 6:4
- Isaiah 41:10
- Romans 8:15-17
- 1 John 3:1

Write in your journal:

"What kind of Father has God shown Himself to be in my life?"

Prayer

Heavenly Father,

Thank You for loving me with a perfect love that never fails. Whether my earthly father was present, absent, or somewhere in between, I know You have always been faithful.

Heal every wound that was created by disappointment, neglect, rejection, or misunderstanding. Replace every lie with Your truth and every fear with Your peace.

Teach fathers to love their daughters well. Help daughters discover their true identity in You. Let every woman reading these pages know that she is chosen, treasured, protected, and deeply loved by her Heavenly Father.

In Jesus' name, Amen.

Chapter 2
Looking for Love

When Wounded Hearts Mistake Validation for Love

"See what great love the Father has lavished on us, that we should be called children of God!" — 1 John 3:1

Every person longs to be loved.

God created us with a desire for intimacy, acceptance, belonging, and connection. Those desires are not sinful. They become dangerous when we begin looking for people to provide what only God can fully satisfy.

When a child's emotional needs go unmet, she often grows into an adult searching for affirmation. If those unmet needs are combined with abuse, neglect, or betrayal, her understanding of love can become painfully distorted.

Instead of asking, "Who will love me?" she begins asking, "What do I have to give to be loved?"

That question has led countless women into unhealthy relationships, toxic cycles, and broken hearts.

My Reflection

Because my emotional needs were never fully met, I began searching for validation in unhealthy places.

I didn't know what genuine love looked like.

As a very young child, I was sexually violated by family members and by people my family trusted. The very people who should have protected me instead became the source of my deepest wounds.

I was only three years old.

At that age, a child cannot understand abuse. She only knows what she experiences. Because those experiences were confused with attention and affection, I began believing something that was never true—that sex was the price of being loved.

The people who were supposed to teach me safety instead taught me fear.

The people who were supposed to protect my innocence instead stole it.

To make matters even more painful, my brother, who was ten years older than me, died at the age of thirteen. That loss left another place of emptiness in my heart.

As I grew older, I found myself looking for validation anywhere I thought I could find it.

I believed that if someone wanted to have sex with me, it meant they loved me.

Looking back, I now understand that I wasn't looking for sex.

I was looking for love.

I was looking for acceptance.

I was looking for someone to tell me I mattered.

I was looking for someone to fill the places that had been broken so early in my life.

But people cannot heal wounds they did not create.

Only Jesus can reach into the deepest places of a wounded heart and restore what was stolen.

The enemy wanted me to believe I was only valuable for what someone could take from me.

God wanted me to know that my value had already been established because I was created in His image.

Healing began when I stopped looking for my identity in other people and started searching for it in Christ.

That journey did not happen overnight, but every step toward God brought me closer to understanding what real love looks like.

Real love never abuses.

Real love never manipulates.

Real love never demands that you sacrifice your dignity to earn acceptance.

Real love protects.

Real love honors.

Real love waits.

Real love reflects the heart of God.

Looking Versus Searching

When we are **looking** for love, we often chase feelings, attention, or approval.

When we are **searching** for God, He teaches us how to recognize genuine love.

Looking asks, *"Who will choose me?"*

Searching asks, *"Lord, who have You created me to be?"*

Looking settles for counterfeits.

Searching waits for God's best.

Reflection Questions

6. What messages about love did I learn as a child?
7. Have I ever confused validation with love?
8. In what ways have my past experiences influenced my relationships?
9. What lies about my worth do I need to surrender to God?
10. What does God's Word say about my identity?

Scripture Study

Read: 1 Corinthians 13:4–8

As you read, ask yourself:

- Does this describe the relationships I've experienced?
- Does this describe the way I love others?
- How does God's love differ from what the world calls love?

Additional Scriptures:

- Psalm 27:10
- Romans 8:38–39
- Isaiah 61:1–3
- Joel 2:25
- 2 Corinthians 5:17

Write in your journal:

"What false belief about love is God asking me to replace with His truth?"

Prayer

Heavenly Father,

Thank You for loving me before I ever knew what love truly was.

You know every wound I have carried, every tear I have cried, and every piece of my heart that has been broken by betrayal and abuse.

Today I surrender every false belief that tells me I must earn love, perform for love, or give away pieces of myself to be accepted.

Teach me to receive the love You freely offer through Jesus Christ. Heal the places that still ache. Restore my identity as Your beloved daughter.

Help me forgive where forgiveness is needed, establish healthy boundaries where wisdom is required, and walk in the freedom You have promised.

May my story become a testimony of Your redeeming power, so that others will know no wound is too deep for Your healing.

In Jesus' name,

Amen.

Chapter 3
Searching for Love

The Difference Between Seeking Affection and Seeking God's Design for Love

Dear Young Tonja,

I know your heart is searching.

You're looking for someone to fill the emptiness left by rejection, abuse, and unanswered questions. Every hug, every compliment, every touch feels like it might finally be what you've been longing for.

But little one, what you're searching for cannot be found in someone's arms. It can only be found in the heart of God.

One day you will discover that affection fades, feelings change, and people disappoint, but God's love remains constant.

You don't have to earn His love.

You don't have to give away pieces of yourself to keep it.

You are already loved because you belong to Him.

One day you will stop searching in broken places and begin resting in the perfect love of your Heavenly Father.

Until then, hold on.

Know that God has you.

With all my love,

Your Older Self
Dr. Tonja Alexander

"Above all, love each other deeply, because love covers a multitude of sins." — 1 Peter 4:8

Every human heart longs to be loved.

The desire to love and be loved is one of the greatest gifts God has placed within us. The problem is not our desire for love; the problem begins when we search for love apart from God's design.

For many years, I wasn't really searching for love.

I was searching for affection.

I didn't know the difference.

Affection made me feel noticed.

Affection made me feel wanted.

Affection made me feel accepted.

But affection alone could never heal my wounded heart.

My Reflection

I was searching for something I had no clue about because I had never been properly shown what love looked like.

Instead of searching for God's design for love, I began seeking what I thought was love, but in reality, it was affection.

Affection is an expression of care or fondness. It can be communicated through words, hugs, kisses, compliments, or physical touch. Healthy affection is a beautiful gift from God.

The problem came when I mistook affection for love.

Because I didn't understand what genuine love looked like or felt like, I accepted almost any form of affection as proof that someone cared about me.

I didn't care if the person I was with only wanted sex.

I only wanted the affection.

I thought affection meant love.

Looking back now, I realize I wasn't chasing relationships.

I was chasing acceptance.

I was chasing validation.

I was chasing the feeling of being wanted because I had never fully experienced the security of unconditional love.

God's design for love is completely different.

Biblical love is rooted in commitment rather than convenience.

It is rooted in sacrifice rather than selfishness.

It is rooted in honor rather than exploitation.

The Bible calls this **agape love,** the unconditional, selfless love that God demonstrates toward us.

Agape love is not based on appearance.

It is not based on feelings.

It is not based on what someone can get from another person.

It chooses to serve.

It chooses to protect.

It chooses to honor.

It chooses to remain faithful.

That kind of love cannot be earned.

It is given.

As I began healing, God showed me something life-changing.

Affection may make you feel loved for a moment.

But only God's love can make you feel secure for a lifetime.

The love I had been searching for was never found in another person's embrace.

It was found in the embrace of my Heavenly Father.

When I finally experienced His unconditional love, I no longer needed affection to tell me I had value.

My identity had already been settled.

I was His daughter.

And that changed everything.

Looking Versus Searching

Looking asks:

"Who will make me feel loved today?"

Searching asks:

"Lord, teach me how to love according to Your Word."

Looking follows emotions.

Searching follows truth.

Looking seeks approval.

Searching seeks God's will.

Looking settles for temporary affection.

Searching discovers everlasting love.

Reflection Questions

11. Have I ever mistaken affection for genuine love?
12. What experiences shaped my understanding of love?
13. Do I seek validation from people more than affirmation from God?
14. What does biblical love require that the world's version of love often ignores?
15. How is God inviting me to experience His unconditional love today?

Scripture Study

Read: 1 Corinthians 13:4–8

As you read, replace the word "love" with "God."

Notice how perfectly He fulfills every description.

Then ask yourself:

- Is this the kind of love I've been seeking?
- Is this the kind of love I'm giving?

Additional Scriptures:

- John 15:13
- Romans 5:8
- Ephesians 3:17–19
- 1 John 4:7–12
- Jeremiah 31:3

Journal Prompt:

"Where have I accepted affection when God desired to give me authentic love?"

Prayer

Heavenly Father,

Thank You for loving me with a love that never changes.

Forgive me for the times I confused attention, affection, and validation with genuine love.

Teach me to recognize the difference between temporary feelings and Your eternal truth.

Heal the places in my heart that still long for approval from people instead of security in You.

Help me receive Your agape love and allow it to transform the way I see myself and the way I love others.

May I never settle for counterfeit love when You have prepared something far greater according to Your perfect will.

In Jesus' name, Amen.

Chapter 4
A Father's Voice

"Death and life are in the power of the tongue…" – Proverbs 18:21

A father's voice is often the first voice that teaches a daughter who she is. Long before she listens to teachers, friends, or even future relationships, she listens to her father. His words can become the foundation upon which she builds her confidence, or the chains that keep her bound to insecurity.

My father was witty. People loved to see him coming because he could make everyone laugh. He had a gift for humor, and his personality could light up a room. But what brought laughter to some often brought pain to others. Words spoken as jokes can leave wounds that last a lifetime.

I remember bringing home my report card one day. Instead of encouragement, my father looked at me and said, "You're so dumb, you flunked walking to school."

He may have laughed after saying it. Others may have laughed too. But I didn't.

I believed him.

From that day forward, school became something I dreaded. I convinced myself that I wasn't smart enough to succeed. I assumed everyone else could understand things that I never would because, in my mind, everyone was smarter than me. One sentence became a belief, and that belief became part of my identity.

Eventually, I dropped out of school.

But God was not finished writing my story.

I earned my G.E.D. Then I began earning certifications in multiple fields of study. Every certificate became proof that my father's words did not define my future. They may have delayed my confidence, but they could not destroy God's purpose for my life.

My father had a commanding voice. He never had to repeat himself. He didn't even call us by name. He would simply yell, "Somebody!" and every child knew that meant all of us needed to come immediately. His voice demanded attention, and what he said carried tremendous weight.

I remember another painful experience during a school shopping trip. My father had taken me, my sister, and the children from his second marriage shopping. I asked if I could have something, and instead of a simple "no," he became angry and began cursing at me.

It wasn't just the rejection that hurt. It was the message behind it that somehow I wasn't worthy of kindness.

One day my father made a statement that pierced my heart. He said that when a man has children by different women, he often loves the children whose mother he loved the most more than the others.

Imagine hearing those words as a daughter.

Imagine believing your father is telling you that you are loved less because of circumstances you had no control over.

Children don't analyze statements like adults do. They absorb them. They personalize them. They carry them into adulthood.

I began to question my worth.

Was I enough?

Was I lovable?

Was there something wrong with me?

Without realizing it, I carried those questions into my relationships, my decisions, and even my understanding of God. The voice of my earthly father became louder than the truth of my Heavenly Father.

Looking back now, I realize that my father probably never understood the weight of his words. What he may have considered casual comments became defining moments in my life. His voice shaped how I viewed myself until I allowed God's voice to reshape my identity.

Many daughters are still living under words spoken decades ago.

"You'll never amount to anything."

"You're just like your mother."

"You're too sensitive."

"You're not good enough."

Those words become internal conversations that play repeatedly throughout life unless they are replaced with God's truth.

Our Heavenly Father speaks differently.

He says we are fearfully and wonderfully made.

He says we are chosen.

He says we are loved.

He says we are His workmanship, created for good works.

The voices of our past may explain our wounds, but they do not have to determine our future.

Today, I no longer define myself by the words spoken over me as a child. I define myself by the Word spoken over me by God. My identity is not rooted in my father's opinions but in my Father's promises.

That change did not happen overnight. It happened one scripture, one prayer, one healing moment, and one act of faith at a time.

Reflection

Every father should understand that his words become the soundtrack playing in his daughter's mind long after she leaves home. She will hear them when she faces challenges, enters relationships, raises her own children, and even when she stands before opportunities God has prepared for her.

Fathers, your voice has the power to build confidence or create insecurity. Speak life. Encourage often. Correct with love. Let your daughters hear words that point them toward their identity in Christ rather than away from it.

Your daughter may forget many of the gifts you bought her, but she will remember how your words made her feel.

Reflection Questions

Take a few moments to answer these questions honestly. There are no right or wrong answers. Invite the Holy Spirit to reveal areas where healing is needed.

16. What words did your father speak over you that you still remember today?
17. Which of those words have shaped the way you see yourself?
18. Have you ever believed something negative about yourself because of what someone else said?
19. How have those beliefs affected your relationships, education, career, or faith?
20. What words from your Heavenly Father do you need to replace those negative beliefs?
21. If you are a father, what words are your children hearing most often from you?
22. What legacy do you want your voice to leave in the lives of your children?

Journal Prompt

Complete the following sentence:

"For years I believed ______________________________, but today God says ______________________________."

Scripture Study

Week 1 Memory Verse

Proverbs 18:21 *"Death and life are in the power of the tongue."*

Reflect:

- How have words brought life into your life?
- How have words brought hurt?
- Which kind of words do you want to become known for speaking?

Read and Meditate

Psalm 139:13–14 You were intentionally created by God.

Ask yourself:

- Do I truly believe I am wonderfully made?
- What keeps me from believing this truth?

Ephesians 2:10 You are God's workmanship.

Write three gifts or strengths God has placed inside you.

Isaiah 43:1 *"Fear not, for I have redeemed you; I have called you by name; you are Mine."*

Notice the contrast: Your earthly father may have called, "Somebody."

Your Heavenly Father calls you by your name.

He knows you personally. He sees your value. He delights in you.

Romans 8:15–17

Study what it means to be adopted into God's family.

Questions:

- What does being God's daughter mean to you?
- How does this change your identity?

Prayer for Healing

Heavenly Father,

Thank You for loving me with a perfect and everlasting love. You know every word that has ever been spoken over my life. You know the ones that encouraged me and the ones that wounded my heart.

Today, I surrender every painful memory to You.

Forgive those who spoke words that damaged my confidence, whether they intended to hurt me or not.

Help me release bitterness, anger, disappointment, and rejection.

Replace every lie I have believed with the truth found in Your Word.

Teach me to see myself the way You see me—chosen, loved, accepted, forgiven, valuable, and wonderfully made.

If I have repeated hurtful words to others, forgive me and help my words become a source of healing instead of pain.

If I am a parent, help me speak life into my children every day. Let my voice encourage, strengthen, and point them toward You.

May Your voice become louder than every voice from my past.

I choose today to believe Your promises over my pain.

In Jesus' name,

Amen.

Father's Challenge

If you are a father, take time this week to intentionally speak life into your daughter.

Tell her:

- I love you.
- I'm proud of you.
- You matter.
- God has a purpose for your life.
- I believe in you.
- You are beautiful inside and out.
- I will always be your father.

Never underestimate the power of your voice.

One conversation can become a lifelong memory.

Choose to make it one that builds rather than breaks.

Daughter's Declaration

Today I choose to believe:

- I am loved by God.
- I am enough because Christ is enough.
- I am fearfully and wonderfully made.
- My past does not define my future.
- My identity is found in Christ.
- I release the painful words spoken over me.
- I receive God's truth over my life.
- I will walk confidently in the purpose God has prepared for me.

"My Father's voice is now greater than my father's voice."

Chapter 5
The Wound of Absence

"A father to the fatherless, a defender of widows, is God in His holy dwelling." – Psalm 68:5

Understanding Father Wounds and Their Impact on Relationships

When people hear the words *father wound,* they often picture a father who was completely absent. While physical absence certainly leaves scars, a father can live in the same house as his daughter and still be emotionally absent.

He may provide food, clothing, and shelter, yet never provide affection.

He may attend every game but never speak words of affirmation.

He may work hard to support his family but never know his daughter's heart.

Presence without connection still creates emptiness.

Many daughters grow up longing for more than a father who is simply there. They long for a father who sees them, hears them, values them, protects them, and loves them in ways they can understand.

As I matured, I came to a difficult but freeing realization.

A father can only teach at the level at which he was taught.

That realization did not excuse the pain I experienced, but it helped me understand it.

My father's parents divorced. I can only imagine the hurt, disappointment, and confusion he carried from his own childhood. Those experiences undoubtedly shaped the man he became and influenced the father he knew how to be.

My father was married four times, including marrying the same wife twice. Looking back, I can see that relationships were complicated for him. Brokenness often leaves patterns that continue until someone chooses to break the cycle.

As I reflected on my own life, I recognized something else.

I was married three times.

That realization caused me to stop pointing only at my father's story and begin examining my own.

Without realizing it, I had carried some of the patterns I witnessed into my own relationships.

Children learn far more from what they observe than from what they are told.

When fathers model unhealthy communication, unresolved anger, disrespect, emotional distance, or instability, daughters may unconsciously accept those behaviors as normal. They may tolerate treatment they should reject because it feels familiar.

That is why healing is so important.

Wounded fathers can unintentionally wound their daughters if their own pain remains unaddressed. But through God's grace, those cycles can be broken. A father's past does not have to become his daughter's future.

I no longer see my father only through the eyes of a wounded daughter. I also see him as a man who had wounds of his own.

That perspective has helped me move toward forgiveness.

Forgiveness does not erase accountability.

Forgiveness does not pretend the hurt never happened.

Forgiveness simply refuses to allow yesterday's pain to control tomorrow's purpose.

The greatest lesson God has taught me is this:

Every generation has an opportunity to stop passing down what wounded them.

Instead of passing down rejection, we can pass down acceptance.

Instead of passing down silence, we can pass down communication.

Instead of passing down anger, we can pass down grace.

Instead of passing down brokenness, we can pass down healing.

That is how generational cycles are broken.

That is how families are restored.

That is how daughters become women who love from a place of healing instead of hurt.

Reflection Questions

23. Was your father physically present, emotionally present, both, or neither? How has that affected you?
24. What relationship patterns did you observe growing up that you later recognized in your own life?
25. Have you ever considered that your father may have been carrying wounds of his own? How does that perspective affect your ability to forgive?

26. Are there unhealthy relationship patterns you want to stop passing on to the next generation?
27. What does forgiveness mean to you? What does it *not* mean?
28. In what ways has God begun healing areas where your family experienced brokenness?

Journal Prompt

Draw two columns. Title the first **"What Was Passed Down to Me"** and the second **"What I Want to Pass Down."** Prayerfully ask God to help you replace unhealthy patterns with godly ones.

Scripture Study

Psalm 68:5

God reveals Himself as "a Father to the fatherless."

Study Questions:

- What does this teach you about God's heart?
- How has God fathered you in seasons when you felt alone?

Ezekiel 36:26

"I will give you a new heart and put a new spirit within you."

Reflect on how God transforms hearts instead of merely changing behaviors.

---

2 Corinthians 5:17

"If anyone is in Christ, he is a new creation."

Write down areas where you desire God to make all things new in your life and relationships.

Joel 2:25

"I will restore to you the years the locust has eaten."

Ask God what restoration could look like in your family story.

Ephesians 4:31–32

Study the connection between forgiveness, kindness, compassion, and healing.

How can forgiving someone set your own heart free?

Prayer for Healing Family Wounds

Heavenly Father,

Thank You for seeing not only my wounds but also the wounds carried by those who came before me.

Today I ask You to heal every place where brokenness has been passed from one generation to another.

Help me understand without excusing what was wrong.

Give me compassion without losing wisdom.

Teach me to forgive as You have forgiven me.

Heal every father wound that has influenced the way I love, trust, communicate, or see myself.

Break every unhealthy cycle that has followed my family for generations.

Let my children and future generations inherit healing instead of hurt, faith instead of fear, and love instead of rejection.

Make me a living example that generational curses can end and generational blessings can begin through Jesus Christ.

In Jesus' name,

Amen.

Father's Challenge

Fathers, your children are learning from more than your words.

They are learning from how you treat their mother.

How you handle disappointment.

How you apologize.

How you forgive.

How you worship.

How you love.

If there are wounds in your own life, invite God to heal them. Your willingness to seek healing may become one of the greatest gifts you ever give your children.

Daughter's Declaration

Today I declare:

- I will not allow yesterday's wounds to define tomorrow's relationships.
- I choose healing over repeating unhealthy patterns.

- I forgive without forgetting the lessons God has taught me.
- I receive God's love as the foundation of my identity.
- My family history does not determine my destiny.
- In Christ, I am becoming a new creation.
- I will leave a legacy of faith, healing, and unconditional love.

"The cycle stops with me because Christ lives in me."

Chapter 6
The Twelve Foundational Years

"Train up a child in the way he should go, and when he is old he will not depart from it." — Proverbs 22:6

Why Birth Through Age Twelve Is Critical for Emotional and Spiritual Development

The first twelve years of a daughter's life are among the most influential years she will ever experience. During this season, she is learning far more than how to walk, talk, read, and write. She is learning what love looks like. She is learning whom she can trust. She is learning where she belongs. She is developing her understanding of relationships, family, security, and ultimately, her perception of God as Father.

While both parents play vital and irreplaceable roles, a father's presence during these formative years provides unique lessons that help shape a daughter's emotional and spiritual foundation.

Love Is First Demonstrated at Home

A little girl learns about love long before she enters her first dating relationship.

She watches.

She listens.

She observes.

She learns what love looks like by watching how her father treats her mother.

When a father speaks kindly to his wife, honors her, listens to her, prays with her, and shows affection and respect, his daughter begins developing healthy expectations for how she deserves to be treated.

She discovers that love is patient.

Love is gentle.

Love protects.

Love serves.

Love sacrifices.

Those early memories become the blueprint she often carries into adulthood.

If conflict, disrespect, fear, or emotional distance become her normal, she may struggle to recognize unhealthy relationships because they feel familiar.

Protection Creates Security

Protection is one of the greatest gifts a father gives his daughter.

When a little girl hears a loud noise or becomes frightened, her first instinct is often to run toward the person she believes can keep her safe.

Many daughters instinctively run behind their father.

His presence becomes her shelter.

His strength becomes her security.

His confidence helps calm her fears.

As she grows, that same protection extends beyond physical safety. A father protects his daughter's heart through guidance, wisdom, discipline, boundaries, and prayer.

He teaches her that she is valuable enough to be protected.

Provision Teaches Responsibility

Children also learn by observing.

A daughter watches her father leave for work, return home, and faithfully provide for his family.

Without realizing it, she is learning responsibility, sacrifice, commitment, and stewardship.

She learns that providing is an expression of love and responsibility.

She sees that healthy families work together and care for one another.

My Reflection

As I have reflected on families throughout my life and ministry, I have come to believe that the first twelve years are foundational.

During those years, a daughter often learns love, protection, and provision by watching her father.

She learns love by seeing how her father treats her mother.

She learns protection by watching her father lead the home with strength, wisdom, and compassion.

She learns provision by watching him work faithfully and care for his family's needs.

When a father is absent—whether physically or emotionally—a daughter may begin looking elsewhere for what she longs to experience.

In many families, the mother courageously steps into multiple roles to provide, protect, and nurture her children. Her sacrifice deserves honor and respect.

At the same time, a daughter may grow up identifying primarily with what she has seen. She may come to believe that she alone must carry every burden, protect everyone around her, and provide for everyone else.

Her understanding of love can become distorted—not because her mother failed her, but because something important was missing.

As she becomes an adult, she may begin searching for love in places that cannot truly satisfy the longing in her heart.

She may seek validation through relationships.

She may mistake attention for affection.

She may confuse control with protection.

She may remain in unhealthy relationships because she is searching for acceptance she never received as a little girl.

Many women become mothers while still carrying the wounds of their own childhood.

When that happens, emotional exhaustion can make it difficult to be fully present with their children.

Some single mothers, longing to be loved themselves, may unintentionally place their focus on finding a relationship before finding healing.

This can sometimes lead to emotionally, verbally, physically, or spiritually abusive relationships that affect the entire family.

Children are watching.

Some sons, longing for guidance, affirmation, and belonging, may begin searching for acceptance outside the home. Sadly, some find it in unhealthy peer groups, criminal activity, or gangs that promise family but often lead to destruction.

This is why healing matters.

When God heals a mother, He blesses her children.

When God restores a father, He strengthens his family.

When parents seek Him together, generations can be changed.

No childhood is beyond God's redemption.

No family is beyond His restoration.

God is able to rebuild foundations that seem broken beyond repair.

The greatest inheritance we can give our children is not wealth.

It is a home where they experience love, protection, truth, grace, and the presence of God.

Reflection Questions

29. What did you learn about love during your first twelve years of life?

30. Who made you feel safe as a child? How has that influenced your relationships today?
31. How did your parents model love, protection, and provision?
32. Have you ever searched for validation, affection, or security in unhealthy places? What were you truly longing for?
33. If you are a parent, what lessons are your children learning by watching you?
34. What kind of legacy do you want to leave for the next generation?

Journal Prompt

Draw three circles labeled **Love, Protection**, and **Provision**. Under each one, write what you received as a child, what you wish you had received, and what you want to pass on to your children or future generations.

Scripture Study

Proverbs 22:6

How can parents intentionally teach children through both words and example?

Deuteronomy 6:6–7

What practical ways can families make God's Word part of everyday life?

Ephesians 6:4

"Fathers, do not provoke your children to anger, but bring them up in the discipline and instruction of the Lord."

Reflect on how discipline and love work together.

---

1 Corinthians 13:4–8

Compare this description of love with what you experienced growing up.

Which qualities were present?

Which qualities do you want to cultivate in your own family?

Psalm 127:3

"Children are a heritage from the Lord."

How does viewing children as God's gift influence the way we raise them?

Prayer for the Next Generation

Heavenly Father,

Thank You for entrusting children to our care. Help us recognize that the early years of their lives are precious opportunities to reflect Your love.

Heal every place where my own childhood has affected the way I parent, love, or trust.

Teach me to model love that is patient and kind, protection that is wise and gentle, and provision that reflects Your faithful care.

Strengthen fathers to lead with humility, integrity, compassion, and courage.

Strengthen mothers who carry heavy responsibilities, and surround them with Your help and support.

Protect our sons from influences that would lead them away from You.

Protect our daughters from believing they must search for love in places that can never satisfy their hearts.

May our homes become places where Your presence is felt, Your Word is honored, and Your love is lived out each day.

Break every unhealthy cycle, and establish a new legacy of faith that will bless generations to come.

In Jesus' name,

Amen.

Parent's Challenge

Whether you are a father, a mother, a grandparent, or a mentor, remember this:

Children learn more from what they see than from what they hear.

Show them how to forgive.

Show them how to pray.

Show them how to love.

Show them how to honor God.

The seeds you plant during the first twelve years can bear fruit for a lifetime.

Daughter's Declaration

Today I declare:

- I am deeply loved by my Heavenly Father.
- My childhood does not define my destiny.

- God is restoring every broken place in my life.
- I choose healthy love over unhealthy patterns.
- I will not seek validation from people when my identity is secure in Christ.
- I will raise the next generation with faith, wisdom, and grace.
- My family story can change because God is writing a new chapter.

"The foundation of my life is no longer built on what was missing—it is built on the unshakable love of my Heavenly Father."

Chapter 7
What Every Daughter Needs

"See what great love the Father has lavished on us, that we should be called children of God!" — 1 John 3:1

Protection, Affirmation, Affection, Instruction, and Presence

Every daughter enters the world with God-given needs that reach far beyond food, clothing, and shelter. She needs to know she is loved, valued, protected, guided, and cherished. While no earthly father is perfect, God designed fathers to reflect His heart by providing security and stability for their daughters.

When these needs are consistently met, a daughter develops confidence, healthy boundaries, and a clearer understanding of God's love. When they are absent, she may spend years searching for what she should have received at home.

Protection

Protection is more than keeping a daughter physically safe.

It is protecting her heart.

It is protecting her innocence.

It is protecting her mind.

It is protecting her future.

Growing up, I longed to know that my father would protect me from being hurt mentally, physically, and emotionally.

Every daughter deserves to know there is someone standing between her and the dangers of this world.

A father's protection teaches his daughter that she is valuable.

She learns she does not have to accept abuse, manipulation, or disrespect because she has seen what healthy protection looks like.

God Himself is our ultimate Protector. Earthly fathers are called to reflect His protective nature by creating an environment where their daughters feel safe enough to grow, dream, and become the women God created them to be.

Affirmation

Words matter.

A father's encouragement becomes a daughter's inner voice.

Every daughter needs to hear:

"I love you."

"I'm proud of you."

"You are beautiful."

"You are smart."

"You are capable."

"You have purpose."

Without affirmation at home, many daughters begin searching for it elsewhere.

I know what it feels like to long for affirmation.

When those words are absent from a father's lips, a daughter may begin believing she must earn approval from others. She may especially seek affirmation from men, confusing attention with acceptance and affection with love.

The desire to be affirmed is not wrong.

God created every daughter to long for love and acceptance.

The danger comes when we seek from people what can only be fully satisfied by God.

Our Heavenly Father has already affirmed our worth.

He calls us His beloved daughters.

Affection

Affection is a beautiful expression of love.

Healthy hugs.

A reassuring hand.

A warm smile.

A gentle embrace.

These expressions communicate safety, acceptance, and belonging.

Every daughter needs appropriate, healthy affection from her father. It reminds her that she is loved simply because she is his daughter—not because she earned it.

Affection should never be confused with manipulation or control.

Healthy affection points a daughter toward security.

Unhealthy affection creates confusion.

Learning the difference is essential.

Instruction

A father teaches by both his words and his example.

He instructs his daughter about integrity.

He teaches responsibility.

He models respect.

He demonstrates how women should be treated.

He points her toward God's truth.

Instruction prepares a daughter for life.

The lessons she learns from her father often influence the choices she makes in friendships, marriage, parenting, and faith.

Wise instruction gives her confidence to navigate life's challenges.

Presence

Perhaps one of the greatest gifts a father can give is simply being present.

Presence means more than living in the same house.

It means listening.

It means attending important moments.

It means asking questions.

It means praying together.

It means putting away distractions and giving undivided attention.

Children spell love with four letters:

T-I-M-E.

A father's presence tells his daughter:

"You matter."

"You're worth my attention."

"I'm here for you."

No amount of money or material gifts can replace the gift of a father's consistent presence.

My Reflection

As I look back over my own life, I realize that every daughter needs to know she is loved.

She needs protection.

She needs affirmation.

She needs healthy affection.

She needs instruction.

She needs presence.

I longed to know that my father would protect me mentally, physically, and emotionally.

I wanted to hear words that reminded me I was beautiful, intelligent, valuable, and loved.

Like many daughters, I found myself searching for affirmation because I had not consistently received it.

I confused affection with love because I desperately wanted to feel accepted.

God eventually revealed that what I had been searching for in people had always been available in Him.

His love never had to be earned.

His affirmation never depended on my performance.

His presence never abandoned me.

Today I know that my greatest identity is not found in the approval of people but in the love of my Heavenly Father.

That truth has transformed my heart and continues to shape the woman I am becoming.

Reflection Questions

35. Which of the five needs—protection, affirmation, affection, instruction, or presence—was most lacking in your childhood?
36. How has that affected your adult relationships?
37. Have you ever confused affection, attention, or validation with genuine love?
38. What words did you long to hear from your father?
39. What words has God spoken about you through His Word?
40. If you are a parent, grandparent, or mentor, how can you intentionally provide these five gifts to the children in your life?

Journal Prompt

Write a letter beginning with these words:

"Dear Little Me, you were always worthy of love because…"

Then write another letter beginning:

"Dear Heavenly Father, thank You for…"

Scripture Study

1 John 3:1

Read this verse several times.

What does it mean to you that God calls you His child?

How does that truth change your identity?

Psalm 91:1–4

Study how God describes His protection.

List the promises found in these verses.

Zephaniah 3:17

Notice how God delights in His children.

How does it feel to know that God rejoices over you with singing?

Proverbs 4:1–9

What instructions does a loving father give his children?

How can you apply these truths today?

Isaiah 41:10

Write every promise God gives in this verse.

Which promise speaks most deeply to your heart?

Prayer for Every Daughter

Heavenly Father,

Thank You for loving me with a perfect and everlasting love.

Thank You for protecting me, even when I did not realize You were watching over me.

Heal every place where I searched for affirmation in people instead of finding my identity in You.

Teach me to recognize the difference between affection and genuine love.

Remind me that I do not have to earn Your acceptance because I already belong to You through Jesus Christ.

Fill every empty place left by disappointment with Your peace, Your truth, and Your presence.

Help fathers everywhere understand the incredible influence they have in the lives of their daughters.

Give them wisdom to protect, affirm, instruct, love, and remain present.

May every daughter know that she is fearfully and wonderfully made, deeply loved, and created for a divine purpose.

In Jesus' name,

Amen.

Father's Challenge

Fathers, your daughter is listening even when she says nothing.

She is watching how you love.

She is watching how you lead.

She is listening to your words.

Tell her often:

"I love you."

"I believe in you."

"I'm proud of you."

"You are beautiful."

"You are smart."

"You are valuable."

"You never have to earn my love."

Those words may become the foundation she stands on for the rest of her life.

Daughter's Declaration

Today I declare:

- I am protected by my Heavenly Father.
- I am deeply loved and fully accepted in Christ.
- I do not have to seek validation from others because God has already affirmed my worth.
- I will no longer confuse affection with love.
- I am beautiful, intelligent, valuable, and created with purpose.
- I will walk confidently in the identity God has given me.

- I will receive God's love and extend it to the next generation.

"Everything I needed, my Heavenly Father has always been, and everything I lacked, He is able to restore."

Chapter 8
Looking for Love in All the Wrong Places

"Beloved, let us love one another, for love is from God..." – 1 John 4:7

Relationships, Attention, Achievement, and Other Substitutions

Every person longs to be loved.

That desire was placed within us by God.

The problem is not the desire for love.

The problem is where we go looking for it.

When the love we longed for was absent during childhood, we often spend adulthood searching for substitutes. Some people seek love through success. Others through money, popularity, alcohol, drugs, or achievement.

My search looked different.

As I got older, I began searching for affection from multiple men.

Looking back, I realize it was never really about them.

It was about me.

I wasn't searching for sex.

I was searching for what I believed love felt like.

I didn't look for love in an alcohol bottle.

I didn't look for it in drugs.

Instead, I became promiscuous.

I slept with men who were emotionally and physically unavailable.

Today, I can honestly admit something that was painful to face.

I didn't truly love myself.

I didn't respect myself.

I didn't recognize my own worth.

When you don't understand your value, you often settle for relationships that never honor the value God placed within you.

I became involved with men who already belonged to someone else.

I wouldn't even call it dating.

I was simply accepting fragments of attention while convincing myself it was love.

Now I understand that I was confusing affection with love because I had never learned the difference.

What Does Love Look Like?

As I reflected on my childhood, I began asking myself a question that changed everything.

What does love actually look like?

My father was a womanizer.

As I mentioned before.

He was married four times and divorced three times.

Without realizing it, I had accepted unhealthy relationship patterns as normal because they were familiar.

I, too, was married three times.

Patterns repeat until someone chooses to break them.

Children often imitate what they observe before they understand what they deserve.

Only God could show me that His design for love looked completely different from what I had experienced.

The Enemy's Strategy

The enemy is content to keep us searching as long as we never discover the truth.

He doesn't always destroy people through obvious sins.

Sometimes he simply keeps them chasing substitutes for God's love.

My search eventually led me into deep emotional pain.

There were seasons when I struggled with suicidal thoughts.

I was hospitalized more than once because the weight of my pain became overwhelming.

Outwardly, I continued searching.

Inwardly, I was broken.

The enemy wanted me to believe my life had no value.

But God had another plan.

Another Broken Relationship

My third husband was twenty-one years older than I was.

One of the greatest struggles in our marriage was the lack of affection.

I was still searching for something no human being could fully provide.

One Sunday morning, while I was on my way to church, he called and deliberately tried to start an argument.

Later that day, when I returned home from worship, he had packed his belongings and left.

He had left me for another man's wife.

I was devastated.

Yet even in that painful moment, God was still working behind the scenes to heal my heart.

Conviction Before the Congregation

Several years later, God entrusted me with the incredible privilege of pastoring a church.

One evening, as I was driving to church, the Holy Spirit spoke clearly to my heart.

I knew I could not stand before God's people and preach His Word while avoiding something He had called me to make right.

The Lord impressed upon my heart that I needed to call the wife of the man with whom I had been involved for seven years.

I was terrified.

I expected anger.

I expected rejection.

I expected her to hang up the phone.

Instead, she extended grace.

She accepted my apology.

Then she asked me one of the most unexpected questions I have ever heard.

"Is there anything I can do for you?"

I completely broke down.

I cried uncontrollably.

How could someone I had hurt respond with such compassion?

Her kindness reflected the heart of Christ.

To this day, I call her the MVP.

Her forgiveness became part of my healing journey.

If you ever read these words, I want to say once again:

Thank you.

Thank you for extending grace when judgment would have been easier.

Thank you for demonstrating forgiveness.

You continue to be in my prayers.

Your compassion became a living picture of God's mercy.

Healing the Little Girl Within

I eventually realized that the woman making unhealthy decisions was still carrying the wounds of the little girl who simply wanted to be loved.

Until that little girl began to heal, I continued searching in places that could never satisfy my heart.

Healing did not begin when I found the right man.

Healing began when I surrendered to the right Father.

Only our Heavenly Father can heal the deepest wounds of our hearts.

Only He can restore what rejection tried to destroy.

Only He can teach us what genuine love looks like.

God is not merely loving.

God is love.

True love is not found in another person.

True love is found in Him.

When we finally experience His unconditional love, we stop begging people to give us what only God can provide.

That is where my healing truly began.

Reflection Questions

41. Where have you looked for love, acceptance, or validation outside of God?

42. Have you ever confused attention, affection, or physical intimacy with genuine love?
43. What unhealthy relationship patterns have you repeated because they felt familiar?
44. Is there someone you need to forgive—or someone from whom you need to seek forgiveness?
45. What is the "little girl" inside you still longing to hear?
46. What would it look like to allow God's love to satisfy the deepest needs of your heart?

Journal Prompt

Complete this sentence:

"For years I searched for love in ______________________________, but today I choose to find my identity in ______________________________."

Then write a letter to your younger self, reminding her that she never had to earn the love that God freely offers.

Scripture Study

1 John 4:7–12

What does this passage teach about the source of true love?

How does knowing that "God is love" reshape your understanding of relationships?

Luke 15:11–24

Read the story of the prodigal son.

Notice how the father responds when his child returns.

What does this reveal about God's willingness to welcome us home after our mistakes?

Romans 8:1

"There is therefore now no condemnation for those who are in Christ Jesus."

How does this promise free you from guilt and shame?

Psalm 147:3

"He heals the brokenhearted and binds up their wounds."

List the wounds you still need to surrender to God.

Pray over each one, asking Him to begin His healing work.

2 Corinthians 5:17

What does it mean to become a "new creation" in Christ?

How can you walk in that new identity each day?

Prayer for Healing and Restoration

Heavenly Father,

Thank You for loving me even when I searched for love in places You never intended for me.

Thank You for Your mercy that reaches beyond my failures and Your grace that welcomes me home.

Forgive me for the choices I made while searching for acceptance, affection, and validation apart from You.

Heal the little girl within me who longed to be loved.

Teach me to receive the unconditional love You have always offered.

Give me the courage to seek forgiveness where I have caused pain and the humility to extend forgiveness to those who have hurt me.

Break every unhealthy pattern that has followed me through relationships.

Restore my heart, renew my mind, and remind me daily that my identity is secure in Christ.

Thank You for proving that no mistake is greater than Your mercy and no wound is beyond Your healing.

In Jesus' name,

Amen.

Healing Challenge

This week, ask God to reveal one area where you have been searching for love outside of Him.

Then take one practical step toward healing.

It may be asking forgiveness.

It may be extending forgiveness.

It may be seeking wise counseling.

It may simply be spending time with your Heavenly Father and allowing Him to speak truth over your life.

Healing begins with one surrendered step at a time.

Daughter's Declaration

Today I declare:

- I no longer have to search for love in people because I have found perfect love in God.
- My past does not define my future.
- I am forgiven, redeemed, and made new through Jesus Christ.
- I release shame and receive God's grace.
- I choose relationships that honor God and honor my worth.
- I am healing from the inside out.
- I am deeply loved by my Heavenly Father.
- I will never again settle for substitutes when God offers me the real thing.

"I stopped looking for love in all the wrong places when I discovered that true love had been pursuing me all along through my Heavenly Father."

Chapter 9
God the Perfect Father

"See what great love the Father has lavished on us, that we should be called children of God!" — 1 John 3:1

Healing Through God's Unconditional Love

For years, I searched for love in people. I searched through relationships. I searched through affection. I searched through acceptance. Yet every place I searched left me emptier than before.

Then I met the One who had been waiting for me all along. When I accepted Jesus Christ as my Lord and Savior, my life changed forever. For the first time, I began to experience unconditional love, not because I had earned it, but because God freely gave it.

That was the beginning of my healing. Notice I said **the beginning**. Healing is a journey. It is not a destination.

My Healing Didn't Happen Overnight

Some people believe that once you accept Christ, every struggle immediately disappears. That was not my experience. Soon after giving my life to Christ, I experienced deep depression. I battled suicidal thoughts. As I shared in an earlier chapter, there were seasons when I found myself in and out of the hospital.

I loved Jesus. Yet I was still hurting. I had to begin unlearning the life I had lived before Christ. I had to let go of premarital sex. I had to stop smoking. I had to stop cursing like a sailor. I had to stop fighting.

Those behaviors did not appear overnight, and they did not disappear overnight. They had become ways of coping with years of pain.

I had experienced sexual abuse. Emotional abuse. Physical abuse. So much anger had built up inside me that it didn't take much to trigger an explosion.

I didn't just need forgiveness. I needed healing.

The Broken Chains

As I spent more time with my Heavenly Father, I could feel chains beginning to break.

Then one day God revealed something that changed my understanding of deliverance.

I said,

"Lord, thank You that my chains have been broken."

Then He showed me something.

Just because chains are broken doesn't always mean they have fallen off.

That revelation stayed with me.

Many of us celebrate when God breaks the chains of addiction, fear, anger, lust, unforgiveness, or rejection.

But sometimes the broken chains are still wrapped around our feet.

They no longer own us.

They no longer have authority over us.

But if we stop walking with God, we can trip over what He has already broken.

Broken chains still attached can become stumbling blocks.

That is why deliverance is not only about freedom.

It is also about daily surrender.

When Old Patterns Return

There came a time when someone from my past reappeared in my life.

Without realizing it, I slowly began spending less time with my Heavenly Father.

The less time I spent in His presence, the more vulnerable I became.

Relationships will either draw us closer to God or pull us farther away from Him.

No person should ever take the place that belongs to God.

When we neglect our relationship with our Heavenly Father, old habits, old wounds, and old temptations often begin knocking on the door again.

That experience reminded me that salvation is the beginning of a relationship, not the end of one.

Knowing the Perfect Father

Once we accept Christ as Lord and Savior, we must intentionally spend time with our Heavenly Father.

Relationships do not grow accidentally.

They grow through time.

Through conversation.

Through trust.

Through obedience.

Through love.

Many of us struggle to understand God as Father because we compare Him to the only father we have ever known.

If your earthly father abandoned you, it may be difficult to believe God will stay.

If your earthly father criticized you, it may be difficult to believe God delights in you.

If your earthly father withheld affection, it may be difficult to receive God's love.

But God is not a better version of our earthly father.

He is the perfect Father.

He never lies.

He never leaves.

He never rejects His children.

He never stops loving us.

The more time I spent with Him, the more He healed the little girl who had spent years searching for love.

He began teaching me what love truly looks like.

His love corrected me without condemning me.

His love disciplined me without rejecting me.

His love restored me without reminding me of my past.

His love transformed me from the inside out.

Today I understand something I never knew as a little girl.

The Father I had been searching for had always been waiting for me.

He wasn't waiting to punish me.

He was waiting to embrace me.

Healing began when I stopped comparing God to imperfect people and allowed Him to reveal Himself as the Perfect Father.

That is where true healing begins for every wounded heart.

Reflection Questions

47. What was your understanding of God as Father before you accepted Christ?
48. Have your experiences with your earthly father made it difficult to trust your Heavenly Father? Why or why not?
49. What "broken chains" are still attached to your life that could become stumbling blocks if you stop walking closely with God?
50. Are there relationships, habits, or distractions pulling you away from your relationship with God?
51. What practical steps can you take this week to spend more intentional time with your Heavenly Father?
52. In what areas have you already seen God's healing in your life?

Journal Prompt

Finish these two statements:

"The little girl inside me still needs…"

"Today my Heavenly Father is teaching me…"

Then write a prayer thanking God for one area where He has already brought healing and asking Him to continue the work He has begun.

Scripture Study

Romans 8:15–17

Read this passage slowly.

What does it mean to you that you have been adopted into God's family?

How does calling God **"Abba, Father"** change your understanding of His love?

John 8:36

"So if the Son sets you free, you will be free indeed."

Reflect on the freedom Christ has already given you.

Are there areas where you need to walk in that freedom more fully?

Philippians 1:6

"He who began a good work in you will carry it on to completion…"

What encouragement does this verse give you when your healing feels incomplete?

James 4:8

"Draw near to God, and He will draw near to you."

List practical ways you can draw closer to God every day.

Psalm 103:1–5

Notice the benefits of belonging to God.

Underline every promise that speaks to healing, forgiveness, restoration, and His unfailing love.

Prayer for Continued Healing

Heavenly Father,

Thank You for loving me before I ever knew how to love myself.

Thank You for sending Jesus to save me and for inviting me into a relationship with You.

Thank You for being the Perfect Father I have always needed.

Forgive me for the times I have drifted away from You and allowed other relationships or distractions to take Your place.

Help me remain close to You every day.

Thank You for breaking the chains that once held me captive.

Now help every broken chain fall completely away so that I may walk freely in the purpose You have for my life.

Continue healing every wound, every memory, and every lie I have believed about myself.

Teach me to receive Your unconditional love and to live as Your beloved daughter.

May my life reflect the freedom, peace, and joy that only You can give.

In Jesus' name,

Amen.

Faith Challenge

This week, intentionally spend time with your Heavenly Father every day.

Read His Word.

Pray honestly.

Sit quietly in His presence.

Write down what He teaches you.

Healing grows in the presence of the Father.

Daughter's Declaration

Today I declare:

- God is my Perfect Father.
- I am deeply loved without condition.
- I am no longer defined by my past.
- The chains of sin and shame have been broken through Jesus Christ.
- I choose to stay close to my Heavenly Father every day.
- I trust His love more than my fears.
- I am being transformed from the inside out.
- The work God has begun in me, He will faithfully complete.

"The Father I was searching for on earth was waiting for me in heaven all along. In His love, I have found my home."

Chapter 10
Breaking the Cycle

"Therefore, if anyone is in Christ, he is a new creation. The old has passed away; behold, the new has come." – 2 Corinthians 5:17

How Women Can Heal and Fathers Can Rebuild Relationships

One of the greatest gifts we can give the next generation is healing.

Every family has a story.

Some stories are filled with joy.

Others are marked by pain, rejection, abandonment, abuse, addiction, divorce, or broken relationships.

The question is not whether we have experienced brokenness.

The question is whether brokenness will end with us.

Healing begins when we become honest.

Before God can heal what is hidden, we must first acknowledge that healing is still needed.

Many of us have learned how to survive.

We know how to smile while hurting.

We know how to attend church while carrying wounds.

We know how to help everyone else while quietly falling apart ourselves.

But surviving is not the same as healing.

God desires more than our survival.

He desires our wholeness.

My Reflection

As women, we can heal.

The first step is coming into the full knowledge that healing is still necessary.

Just because the chains have been broken does not mean the healing process is complete.

Healing comes through the Word of God, through prayer, through obedience, and through spending time in the presence of our Heavenly Father.

For a long time, I believed that breaking the cycle was enough.

Then God gave me a different perspective.

When something is broken, it can often be put back together.

But when something is completely consumed by fire, it cannot return to its former state.

That is what I want God to do in my life.

I don't simply want Him to break unhealthy patterns.

I want Him to destroy them.

I want every lie, every wound, every unhealthy relationship pattern, every fear, every spirit of rejection, and every generational cycle to be consumed by the fire of His Holy Spirit.

When God's refining fire transforms us, we are no longer the same person.

We become new creations.

The old life loses its power because God has made something entirely new.

That relationship we develop with God—through His Word, through prayer, and through time in His presence—is what ignites that holy fire.

His truth burns away deception.

His love burns away rejection.

His peace burns away fear.

His grace burns away shame.

His presence sets us free.

Rebuilding Relationships

Healing also changes the way we see people.

As God healed my heart, I realized I could begin rebuilding my relationship with my natural father.

Rebuilding does not always mean everything becomes perfect.

Sometimes healing changes you even when the other person never changes.

Your father may never apologize.

He may never acknowledge the pain he caused.

He may never say,

"I'm sorry for not protecting you."

"I'm sorry for not being emotionally present."

"I'm sorry for not covering you."

"I'm sorry for not loving you the way you deserved."

Those words may never come.

That reality is painful.

But your healing cannot depend upon another person's apology.

Through your relationship with your Heavenly Father, you can choose forgiveness even when reconciliation looks different than you hoped.

Forgiveness does not require another person's participation.

It is an act of obedience that frees your own heart.

As I grew in my relationship with God, I realized something beautiful.

Everything I longed to hear from my earthly father, my Heavenly Father had already spoken through His Word.

He is my Protector.

He is my Provider.

He is my Shepherd.

He is my Comforter.

He is my Defender.

He loves me with an everlasting love.

Because of Him, I no longer live waiting for an apology that may never come.

I live resting in the love that has never failed me.

A New Legacy Begins Today

Perhaps you are reading this book while carrying wounds that have existed for decades.

Perhaps your father has passed away.

Perhaps reconciliation is no longer possible.

Or perhaps your father is still living, and there is hope for a restored relationship.

Whatever your situation, know this:

God specializes in new beginnings.

Your family history is not your final destination.

Your pain does not have to become your children's inheritance.

Through Jesus Christ, a new legacy can begin today.

The cycle ends here.

Not because you are strong enough.

But because God is faithful enough.

Reflection Questions

53. What unhealthy patterns have you recognized in your family that you do not want to pass on?
54. Are you merely surviving, or are you allowing God to bring complete healing?
55. What does it mean to you to allow God to completely destroy unhealthy cycles instead of simply breaking them?
56. Is there someone you need to forgive, even if they never apologize?
57. How has your relationship with your Heavenly Father changed your understanding of forgiveness?

58. What legacy do you want your children, grandchildren, or those you mentor to inherit?

Journal Prompt

Write two lists.

The first is titled **"What Ends With Me."**

The second is titled **"What Begins With Me."**

Pray over each list and ask God to establish a new legacy through your life.

Scripture Study

2 Corinthians 5:17

Read this verse slowly.

What does becoming a "new creation" mean in your daily life?

How does it give you hope for breaking unhealthy patterns?

Isaiah 43:18–19

"Forget the former things… See, I am doing a new thing!"

What new thing do you believe God wants to do in your life?

Joel 2:25

God promises restoration.

What areas of your life do you need Him to restore?

Ephesians 4:31–32

Study how forgiveness, kindness, and compassion work together.

How can forgiving someone free your own heart?

Romans 12:2

"Be transformed by the renewing of your mind."

What thoughts or beliefs does God want to replace with His truth?

Prayer for Breaking the Cycle

Heavenly Father,

Thank You for loving me enough to heal what has been broken for generations.

Today I surrender every wound, every painful memory, every unhealthy pattern, and every lie I have believed about myself.

I ask You not only to break the cycle but to destroy every stronghold that has kept my family bound.

Let the fire of Your Holy Spirit burn away fear, rejection, bitterness, shame, unforgiveness, and everything that opposes Your will for my life.

Help me become the woman You created me to be.

Teach me to forgive, even when I never receive an apology.

Teach me to love, even after experiencing hurt.

Teach me to trust You completely.

Strengthen fathers who desire to rebuild relationships with their daughters.

Give them humility, wisdom, and courage to lead with love.

May healing begin in every home represented by those reading these pages.

Let my life become evidence that generational brokenness can end through Jesus Christ.

I declare that my children and future generations will inherit faith instead of fear, healing instead of hurt, and hope instead of despair.

In Jesus' mighty name,

Amen.

Father's Challenge

If you are a father, today is an opportunity to begin again.

You cannot rewrite yesterday, but by God's grace you can influence tomorrow.

If you have wounded your daughter, have the courage to acknowledge it.

A sincere apology does not diminish your strength—it demonstrates humility and love.

If reconciliation is possible, pursue it with patience, honesty, and prayer.

The relationship may not be restored overnight, but every step toward healing matters.

Daughter's Declaration

Today I declare:

- The cycle of brokenness ends with me.

- I choose healing over hurt.
- I choose forgiveness over bitterness.
- I choose God's truth over the lies of my past.
- I am no longer waiting for an apology to experience freedom.
- My Heavenly Father is my Protector, Provider, and unfailing source of love.
- Through Christ, I am creating a new legacy for generations to come.
- I will walk in freedom, purpose, and peace all the days of my life.

"The cycle did not end because I became stronger. The cycle ended because I surrendered to the One whose love is stronger than every wound."

Chapter 11
A Letter to Fathers

"Fathers, do not provoke your children to anger, but bring them up in the discipline and instruction of the Lord." – Ephesians 6:4

Practical Guidance for Raising Daughters with Purpose and Confidence

Fathers,

You may never fully realize the influence you have in your daughter's life.

To you, she may simply be your little girl.

To her, you are the first man she will ever love.

You are the first man who teaches her how she should be treated.

You are the first voice that helps shape her confidence.

You are the first example of protection.

You are the first example of provision.

You are the first example of love.

Whether you realize it or not, your daughter is watching you every day.

She is listening to your words.

She is watching how you treat her mother.

She is learning what she should expect from every relationship that follows.

That is why your presence matters.

Your words matter.

Your affection matters.

Your time matters.

Your love matters.

Dear Father,

I know you may not have realized that being physically present without being emotionally present could leave such a deep wound in your little girl's heart.

She wasn't looking for perfection.

She was looking for connection.

She was searching for something she couldn't even name because she had never experienced it.

She wanted your attention.

She wanted your affection.

She wanted your encouragement.

She wanted to know she mattered.

Do you remember when your little girl kept finding herself in one unhealthy relationship after another?

Perhaps you wondered,

"What does she see in him?"

"Why would she stay with someone who doesn't work?"

"Why would she allow someone to call her out of her name?"

"Why would she settle for someone who doesn't value her?"

The answer may be more heartbreaking than you realize.

She wasn't looking for him.

She was looking for what she hoped he would give her.

Love.

Approval.

Protection.

Affection.

Acceptance.

She was searching for what she never fully received.

Because she had never experienced healthy love consistently, she struggled to recognize unhealthy love.

She accepted less because she didn't know she deserved more.

That is why I am writing this letter.

Not to condemn you.

But to remind you that today is another opportunity to make a difference.

To Every Father Raising a Daughter

Especially to those raising little girls between birth and twelve years old:

These years matter.

These years are precious.

These years help shape how your daughter will see herself, others, and even God.

Hold her hand.

Read to her.

Pray with her.

Laugh with her.

Listen to her stories.

Attend her school events.

Celebrate her victories.

Comfort her disappointments.

Be present not only physically but emotionally.

Embrace your little girl.

Tell her she is beautiful.

Tell her she is intelligent.

Tell her she is strong.

Tell her she is kind.

Tell her she is loved.

Tell her she is fearfully and wonderfully made.

Tell her she has purpose.

Tell her she is precious in God's sight.

Protect her heart.

Protect her innocence.

Protect her dreams.

Protect her confidence.

Help her know she never has to earn your love.

Because when a daughter grows up hearing these truths from her father, she is less likely to spend her adult life searching for someone else to tell her who she already knows she is.

Build her confidence now.

Help her discover her identity now.

Teach her whose she is before the world tells her who she should be.

A confident daughter doesn't need to chase acceptance.

She doesn't have to compete for attention.

She doesn't have to compromise her values to fit into someone else's circle.

She already knows who she is.

She knows she belongs.

She knows she is loved.

She knows she has purpose.

She is complete because her identity is rooted in Christ.

As I often say:

She doesn't have to fit into anyone else's circle… because she is the circle.

Love Always,

Your Little Girl

Reflection Questions

For Fathers

59. If your daughter described your relationship today, what do you think she would say?

60. Are you emotionally present, or only physically present?
61. What encouraging words have you spoken to your daughter this week?
62. How do your actions teach your daughter what love looks like?
63. What changes can you make today to strengthen your relationship with your daughter?

For Daughters

1. What words did you long to hear from your father?
2. How have your father's actions shaped your view of yourself?
3. Have you allowed God's truth to replace painful messages from your past?
4. What kind of legacy do you want to leave for future generations?

Journal Prompt

Fathers:

Write a letter to your daughter telling her everything you hope she knows about herself.

Daughters:

Write a letter to your younger self reminding her that she has always been deeply loved by God.

Scripture Study

Ephesians 6:4

How can fathers raise their children with both truth and grace?

What does it mean to nurture instead of discourage?

Psalm 127:3–5

What responsibility comes with viewing children as God's gift?

How can fathers faithfully steward that gift?

Proverbs 31:25–31

Which character qualities should fathers encourage in their daughters?

How can fathers praise qualities that go beyond outward beauty?

Psalm 139:13–18

Read these verses aloud.

Write down every truth God says about His creation.

How can fathers reinforce these truths in their daughters' lives?

Numbers 6:24–26

Read this blessing over your daughter every day this week.

Pray it with intention and love.

Prayer for Fathers and Daughters

Heavenly Father,

Thank You for entrusting fathers with the incredible privilege of raising daughters.

Give fathers wisdom to lead with humility, compassion, patience, and love.

Help them become living examples of Your heart.

Teach them to speak life, encourage often, protect faithfully, and love unconditionally.

Heal every father-daughter relationship that has been damaged by misunderstanding, absence, harsh words, or broken trust.

Give daughters the confidence to know they are deeply loved—not because of what they do, but because of who they are in Christ.

Help every little girl grow into a woman who understands her worth, walks in her purpose, and refuses to settle for anything less than the love You desire for her.

May fathers point their daughters toward You, the Perfect Father, whose love never fails.

In Jesus' name,

Amen.

Father's Challenge

This week, intentionally create one meaningful memory with your daughter.

Put away your phone.

Turn off the television.

Look her in the eyes.

Tell her:

"I love you."

"I'm proud of you."

"You are beautiful."

"You are smart."

"You are kind."

"You are valuable."

"You have purpose."

Then ask her one simple question:

"Is there anything you wish you could tell me that I've never asked?"

Listen without interrupting.

Your willingness to listen may begin healing conversations that last a lifetime.

Daughter's Declaration

Today I declare:

- I am deeply loved by my Heavenly Father.
- I am fearfully and wonderfully made.
- I do not need to earn acceptance because I already belong to God.
- I know my value because my Creator defines my worth.
- I will not settle for relationships that dishonor who God created me to be.
- I will walk confidently in my purpose.
- I will leave a legacy of faith, strength, and unconditional love.

"I no longer search for someone to tell me who I am. My Heavenly Father has already spoken, and His Word is enough. I am complete not because the world completed me, but because Christ made me whole."

Chapter 12
A Letter to Daughters

"For I know the plans I have for you," declares the Lord, "plans to prosper you and not to harm you, plans to give you hope and a future." — Jeremiah 29:11

Finding Your Worth in Christ Rather Than in the Approval of Others

Dear Daughter,

If I could sit across from you today, hold your hand, and tell you one thing, it would be this:

You are already enough.

Not because of your accomplishments.

Not because someone chose you.

Not because someone complimented you.

Not because you are in a relationship.

You are enough because God created you, loves you, and calls you His daughter.

For years, I searched for my worth in places that could never truly satisfy my heart.

I searched through relationships.

I searched through affection.

I searched through approval.

I searched through people.

But every search left me emptier because I was asking people to give me something that only God could provide.

I don't want you to spend years making the same mistake I made.

Dear Daughters,

Stop searching for approval from people.

Begin looking to your Heavenly Father for your worth.

Everything you have been searching for can be found in Him.

You will find acceptance in Him.

You will find peace in Him.

You will find purpose in Him.

You will find unconditional love in Him.

Seek Him.

Spend time with Him.

Talk with Him every day.

Read His Word.

Listen for His voice.

Allow Him to heal the little girl inside you.

Don't only go to God when you need Him.

Relationships are not built on constant requests.

Real relationships are built on love, trust, communication, and time together.

Sometimes, instead of saying,

"Father, what can You do for me?"

Ask Him,

"Father, what can I do for You?"

That simple question changes your heart.

It moves your focus from receiving to surrendering.

Your Heavenly Father is not looking for perfection.

He is looking for relationship.

He delights in spending time with you.

He already knows every tear you've cried.

Every disappointment you've experienced.

Every mistake you've made.

Every dream you've buried.

Every prayer you've whispered.

Yet He still loves you completely.

He has never stopped loving you.

He never will.

The Bible tells us that He will never leave you nor forsake you.

Even when people walk away…

He remains.

Even when relationships fail…

He remains.

Even when your heart is broken…

He remains.

Even when you feel forgotten…

He remains.

Jeremiah 29:11 reminds us that God knows the plans He has for us.

He already knows your purpose.

He already knows your future.

He already knows the woman He created you to become.

Now, daughters…

It's time for you to know Him.

Not just know about Him.

Know Him personally.

Know His voice.

Know His heart.

Know His promises.

Know His love.

When you know Him, you no longer have to chase what the world offers because you have discovered the One who is more than enough.

The little girl who spent years looking for love has now become a woman who has found perfect love in her Heavenly Father.

That is my prayer for you.

May you never again settle for substitutes when God offers you Himself.

Love Always,

A Daughter Who Finally Found Her Father

Reflection Questions

5. Where have you been seeking your worth or approval?
6. What does it mean to you to be called God's daughter?
7. How has your relationship with your Heavenly Father changed over the course of reading this book?
8. What is one lie about yourself that you are ready to replace with God's truth?

9. How can you intentionally spend more time with God this week?
10. If a young girl asked you what true love looks like, how would you answer after reading this book?

Journal Prompt

Write a letter to your Heavenly Father.

Tell Him everything that is on your heart.

Then sit quietly and read one chapter of Scripture, asking Him to speak to you through His Word.

Write down what you believe He is teaching you.

Scripture Study

Jeremiah 29:11–13

Read the entire passage, not just verse 11.

Notice that God not only has plans for His people but also invites them to seek Him with all their hearts.

Ask yourself:

- Am I truly seeking God?
- What distractions keep me from pursuing Him wholeheartedly?

Matthew 6:33

"Seek first the kingdom of God and His righteousness, and all these things will be added to you."

What changes when God becomes your first priority instead of your last resort?

Romans 8:38–39

Study the verses describing God's inseparable love.

List everything that cannot separate you from His love.

Psalm 27:10

"Though my father and mother forsake me, the Lord will receive me."

How does this promise bring comfort to those who have experienced rejection?

John 15:9

"As the Father has loved Me, so have I loved you. Now remain in My love."

What practical habits help you remain in God's love every day?

Prayer of Surrender

Heavenly Father,

Thank You for pursuing me even when I was searching for love in all the wrong places.

Thank You for never giving up on me.

Today I surrender my need for the approval of people.

I choose to find my identity in You alone.

Teach me to know You more deeply.

Help me desire Your presence more than the praise of others.

Heal every wounded place in my heart.

Replace rejection with acceptance.

Replace fear with peace.

Replace shame with grace.

Replace loneliness with the assurance that I am never alone because You are always with me.

Teach me to love You with all my heart, all my soul, all my mind, and all my strength.

May my life reflect Your love to every person I meet.

Thank You for calling me Your daughter.

Thank You for giving me hope.

Thank You for giving me purpose.

Thank You for loving me perfectly.

In Jesus' name,

Amen.

Daughter's Challenge

For the next thirty days, spend intentional time with your Heavenly Father.

Read His Word before you read social media.

Pray before you make major decisions.

Write down one thing He teaches you each day.

Instead of asking only, *"Lord, what can You do for me?"* also ask,

"Father, how can I love You and serve others today?"

As you spend time with Him, you will begin to recognize His voice more clearly and His love more deeply.

Daughter's Declaration

Today I declare:

- I am a beloved daughter of God.
- My worth is found in Christ, not in the approval of others.
- I no longer have to search for love because I have found perfect love in my Heavenly Father.
- I am fearfully and wonderfully made.
- I am chosen, accepted, forgiven, and redeemed.
- God's plans for my life are good.

- I will seek God with my whole heart.
- I will walk confidently in my purpose.
- I am complete because Christ has made me whole.

"I spent years searching for love, only to discover that Love had been waiting for me all along. My Heavenly Father knew my name before I ever knew His heart. Today, I stop searching, I stop striving, and I simply rest in the perfect love of my Father. I have found my home in Him."

The Father's Embrace

"See what great love the Father has lavished on us, that we should be called children of God! And that is what we are!"
– 1 John 3:1

Before you close this book, I want you to do one thing.

Stop.

Be still.

Take a deep breath.

Now, close your eyes for just a moment and imagine yourself as the little girl you once were.

The little girl who longed to be seen.

The little girl who wanted to be protected.

The little girl who wanted someone to tell her she was beautiful, valuable, and enough.

The little girl who searched for love in all the wrong places because she didn't know what true love looked like.

Now imagine your Heavenly Father gently walking toward her.

He isn't coming with condemnation.

He isn't coming with anger.

He isn't coming to remind her of her mistakes.

He comes with open arms.

He kneels beside her.

He wipes away every tear.

He lifts her head.

He looks into her eyes and says:

"My precious daughter...

I have always loved you.

I have always seen you.

I have always known your name.

You were never forgotten.

You were never abandoned by Me.

I was with you through every tear, every disappointment, every heartbreak, and every lonely night.

I know the pain you've carried.

I know the questions you've asked.

I know the wounds you've tried to hide.

Bring them to Me.

You don't have to carry them anymore.

I am your Protector.

I am your Provider.

I am your Peace.

I am your Healer.

I am your Father.

You no longer have to search for love because My love has been pursuing you all along.

Come to me, My daughter.

Rest in My embrace.

You are Mine."

Today, I pray that every chain has broken and fallen off.

That every lie has been replaced with God's truth.

That every wound has begun to heal.

That every reader who once searched for love now rests securely in the everlasting love of the Father.

As you leave these pages, remember this:

You are not leaving empty.

You are leaving loved.

You are not leaving broken.

You are leaving healed.

You are not leaving rejected.

You are leaving accepted.

You are not leaving alone.

You are leaving in the embrace of your Heavenly Father.

A Final Prayer

Heavenly Father,

Thank You for meeting me here.

Thank You for loving me before I ever knew how to love myself.

Thank You for never giving up on me.

Today I receive Your love.

I receive Your forgiveness.

I receive Your healing.

I receive my identity as Your daughter.

From this day forward, I choose to walk in freedom instead of fear, purpose instead of pain, and faith instead of doubt.

Help me become a reflection of Your love to everyone I meet.

May my life tell the story that You restore broken hearts, redeem wounded souls, and make all things new.

In Jesus' name,

Amen.

The Father's Blessing

"The Lord bless you and keep you;

The Lord make His face shine upon you and be gracious to you;

The Lord turn His face toward you and give you peace."

– Numbers 6:24–26

Go forward knowing this truth:

You are loved.

You are chosen.

You are healed.

You are enough.

You are His.

The End… or rather, the Beginning.

Conclusion

Stop Looking for Love and Start Searching for the One Who Is Love

"Whoever does not love does not know God, because God is love." – 1 John 4:8

If you've made it to the end of this book, I want to first thank you for allowing me to share my heart and my journey with you.

Perhaps you saw pieces of yourself in my story.

Maybe you recognized your own pain, your own disappointments, or even your own search for love.

Or maybe, for the first time, you realized why you've spent so many years looking for something that always seemed just out of reach.

I understand.

I was that little girl.

I became that woman.

I spent years looking for love in places that could never satisfy the deepest longing of my heart.

I searched through relationships.

I searched through affection.

I searched through marriage.

I searched through approval.

I searched through acceptance.

I searched through people.

And every time I thought I had found love, I discovered I had only found another substitute.

You have been looking long enough.

How much longer will you search for something that has never truly satisfied your soul?

How many more relationships?

How many more disappointments?

How many more tears?

How many more broken hearts?

There comes a time when you grow weary of searching.

There comes a time when you realize you have been looking in all the wrong directions.

Today, I invite you to stop looking for love and start searching for the One who **is** love.

Our Heavenly Father is not simply loving.

He is Love.

His love is not based on your performance.

His love is not based on your past.

His love is not based on your mistakes.

His love is not based on whether someone else chose you.

His love is unconditional.

His love is faithful.

His love is everlasting.

His love is perfect.

The Word of God teaches us that true love is unconditional, selfless, and sacrificial. It seeks the good of others before itself. It does not manipulate. It does not abuse. It does not abandon. It does not keep score.

That is the love our Heavenly Father has for you.

Perhaps your earthly father could not give you everything you needed.

Perhaps he gave what he knew.

Perhaps he carried wounds of his own.

Perhaps he was absent.

Perhaps he was present but emotionally unavailable.

Whatever your story may be, your future does not have to be defined by your past.

Your Heavenly Father is inviting you into a relationship that no human being can replace.

He wants to heal the little girl who still cries silently inside you.

He wants to restore your confidence.

He wants to remove your shame.

He wants to teach you what healthy love truly looks like.

He wants you to know that you have always been worthy—not because of what you have done, but because of whose you are.

You are His daughter.

You are chosen.

You are loved.

You are accepted.

You are forgiven.

You are redeemed.

You are fearfully and wonderfully made.

You have purpose.

You have value.

You have a future.

As you close this book, my prayer is not simply that you remember my story.

My prayer is that you begin living yours differently.

May you stop searching for approval and begin resting in God's acceptance.

May you stop chasing affection and begin receiving His unconditional love.

May you stop settling for relationships that diminish your worth and begin believing what God says about you.

May fathers choose to become emotionally present.

May daughters discover their identity in Christ.

May families be restored.

May generational cycles be broken.

May forgiveness replace bitterness.

May healing replace hurt.

May hope replace despair.

And may every little girl who once wondered, **"Am I enough?"** finally hear the voice of her Heavenly Father saying,

"You have always been enough because you have always been Mine."

If you are reading this today and you have never fully surrendered your life to Jesus Christ, know that this is where true healing begins. He is not waiting to condemn you; He is inviting you into His family. His arms are open, His grace is sufficient, and His love is greater than every mistake, every wound, and every regret.

The journey that began with a little girl looking for love does not end with disappointment.

It ends with a daughter who has found her home in the heart of her Heavenly Father.

So today…

Stop looking.

Start seeking.

Seek the One who has been seeking you all along.

Because when you find Him…

You will finally discover the love you have been searching for your entire life.

Love Always,

Dr. Tonja Alexander

Final Reflection Questions

11. What is the greatest lesson God has taught you through this journey?
12. What wounds has God begun to heal in your heart?

13. Are you still looking for love in places that cannot satisfy, or have you begun resting in God's love?
14. What relationship do you need to surrender to God today?
15. What generational cycle ends with you?
16. How will your life look different because you now understand your identity in Christ?

Final Journal Prompt

Write a letter to yourself dated one year from today.

Describe the woman you believe God is calling you to become.

Then write a second letter titled:

"Dear Heavenly Father..."

Tell Him why you choose to stop looking for love and start walking with Him.

Final Scripture Study

1 Corinthians 13:4–8

Read the passage slowly.

Compare God's definition of love with the relationships you have experienced.

Ask yourself:

- Which qualities have I experienced?
- Which qualities do I now desire in my relationships?
- How can I reflect Christ's love to others?

Jeremiah 29:11–13

Notice that God not only has plans for your life—He also promises that when you seek Him with all your heart, you will find Him.

Romans 8:38–39

Meditate on the truth that nothing can separate you from God's love.

Read these verses aloud every day for one week.

Psalm 23

Read this chapter as if your Heavenly Father is speaking directly to you.

Notice every way He provides, protects, leads, restores, and comforts His children.

Final Prayer

Heavenly Father,

Thank You for meeting me in the middle of my search.

Thank You for never giving up on me, even when I wandered far from You.

Today I choose to stop searching for love in places that can never satisfy my soul.

I choose You.

Heal every wound.

Restore every broken place.

Renew my mind.

Strengthen my faith.

Teach me to love as You love.
Help me walk confidently as Your daughter, knowing that I am chosen, accepted, forgiven, and deeply loved.

Use my story to encourage someone else who is still searching.

May my life always point others toward the only perfect love that never fails.

In Jesus' name,

Amen.

Final Declaration

Today I declare:

- I am no longer searching for love—I have found it in my Heavenly Father.
- I am chosen.
- I am accepted.
- I am forgiven.
- I am healed.
- I am redeemed.
- I am fearfully and wonderfully made.
- I am complete in Christ.
- I am loved with an everlasting love.
- I know who I am because I know whose I am.

"I spent years looking for love, only to discover that Love had been looking for me all along. I am no longer searching—I am home."

A Letter to the Little Girl Within

Dear Little Girl,

I know you've been searching for love in all the wrong places.

I know you've cried silent tears that no one ever saw.

I know you've wondered if you were enough, if you were worthy, and if anyone would ever truly love you.

I know you've carried wounds that were never your fault.

But today, I want you to know something that will change your life forever.

Stop searching for love in people who cannot give you what only God can provide.

Look to your Heavenly Father, for **He is Love**.

He has always loved you.

He has always seen you.

He has always known your name.

He has always had a purpose for your life.

Do not allow your past to dictate your future.

Your past may explain your pain, but it does not define your purpose.

You are not what happened to you.

You are who God says you are.

You are fearfully and wonderfully made.

You are chosen.

You are accepted.

You are forgiven.

You are beautiful.

You are valuable.

You are deeply loved.

Allow your Heavenly Father to heal every broken place in your heart.

Allow Him to restore what was stolen.

Allow Him to replace rejection with acceptance, fear with peace, shame with grace, and hurt with hope.

You don't have to keep searching anymore.

You have found your way home.

Your Heavenly Father has been waiting for you with open arms all along.

Walk confidently into the beautiful future He has prepared for you.

And whenever you begin to doubt your worth, remember this one truth:

You have always been enough because you have always belonged to Him.

With love and prayers,

Dr. Pastor Tonja Alexander

Dear Three-Year-Old Tonja,

I see you.

I know you're scared, confused, and carrying pain that no three-year-old should ever have to bear. I know you don't understand why the people who were supposed to protect you became the ones who hurt you. None of this is your fault.

You are not dirty.

You are not damaged.

You are not to blame.

You are a precious little girl created in the image of God, and what happened to you did not change your value one bit.

I know you're searching for someone to tell you that you're beautiful, worthy, and enough. I know you'll spend years believing that if someone wanted you, they loved you. But one day you'll discover the greatest truth of all—you never had to earn love because God loved you before you ever took your first breath.

One day you'll learn that what was taken from you cannot determine who you become.

Your pain will not be the end of your story.

God will heal your broken heart.

He will wipe away your tears.

He will give you beauty for ashes.

He will use your voice to help women and little girls who have walked through the same darkness you once knew.

The enemy wanted your silence.

God has chosen your testimony.

The little girl who once cried in secret will become a woman who stands in the light and tells others that healing is possible through Jesus Christ.

So hold on, little one.

The road ahead won't always be easy, but God will never leave you. He will carry you when you're too weak to walk. He will become the Father who never abandons His daughter.

And one day, you won't just survive.

You'll help others live.

With all my love,

Your Older Self
Dr. Tonja Alexander

To My Spiritual Mother, Pastor Helen Davis,

There are people God places in our lives for a season, and then there are those He places in our lives to help shape our destiny.

You are one of those people.

Thank you for stepping into my life and becoming the spiritual support, I so desperately needed as a young mother of four.

Looking back, I realize God knew exactly what I needed when He placed you in my life.

(LOL... I just didn't know it at the time!)

There I was—cussing, smoking those Newports, and living life my way.

And there you were...

With that loving but firm voice saying,

"Put those things down... and stop all that cussing!"

Many people thought you were mean.

I knew better.

I understood that your correction came from a heart of love.

You weren't trying to control me.

You were trying to help me become the woman God had already called me to be.

You saw beyond my struggles.

You saw beyond my attitude.

You saw beyond my mistakes.

You saw God's purpose in me before I could see it for myself.

Thank you for loving me enough to correct me.

Thank you for praying for me.

Thank you for believing in me.

Thank you for encouraging me to keep growing in Christ.

Most of all…

Thank you for never giving up on me.

Your prayers, your wisdom, your correction, and your unconditional love have helped shape the woman, minister, pastor, and author I am today.

I will forever be grateful that God allowed our paths to cross.

May He continue to bless you abundantly for every life you have touched including mine.

With love, honor, and gratitude,

Dr. Pastor Tonja

You were [illegible] to help me become the woman God had already called me to be.

You saw [illegible].

You saw me, and my [illegible].

[illegible]

You saw God's purpose for me before I could see it for myself.

Thank you for [illegible].

Thank you for praying for me.

Thank you for believing in me.

Thank you for encouraging me to keep growing in Christ.

Most of all,

Thank you for [illegible].

Your prayers, your wisdom, [illegible] the woman [illegible] I am today.

I will never [illegible].

May He continue to bless you [illegible].

With love, honor, and gratitude,

Dr. Pastor Tonja

To My Beloved Children,

Life has not always been easy growing up with a young mother who was searching for love, acceptance, and healing.

There were times when I didn't have all the answers. There were moments when I made mistakes while trying to find my own way. Yet through it all, God's grace carried us.

I want each of you to know how deeply grateful I am that our Heavenly Father entrusted you to me. Each one of you is a precious gift, uniquely created by God with a purpose that only you can fulfill.

Never compare yourself to anyone else. God created you to be exactly who He intended you to be. Walk boldly in your gifts, pursue His purpose for your life, and trust Him with your future.

Remember that your identity is not found in the opinions of others but in Christ alone. You never have to search for your worth because your Heavenly Father has already declared that you are loved, chosen, and fearfully and wonderfully made.

My prayer is that you will always seek God first, love Him with all your heart, and allow Him to direct every step you take.

No matter where life leads you, always remember that God has so much more in store for you than you could ever imagine.

I am so proud to be your mother.

Thank you for loving me, growing with me, and extending grace to me as I learned, healed, and became the woman God called me to be.

I love each of you more than words can express, and I will always be cheering you on.

May God's favor, peace, protection, and unconditional love surround you all the days of your lives.

With all my love,

Your Mother

Dr. Pastor Tonja Alexander

Dedication to My Firstborn

To My Oldest Daughter, Dr. Minister I-Isha Hudson,

My firstborn.

My right hand.

My protector.

My cheerleader.

My caregiver.

My chef.

My greatest supporter.

Words could never fully express how grateful I am for the woman you have become.

From a very young age, life required you to grow up much faster than you should have. You stepped into the role of a second mother to your siblings without ever being asked. You carried responsibilities that many adults struggle to carry, and you did it with strength, grace, and unconditional love.

Thank you.

Thank you for standing beside me when life became difficult.

Thank you for protecting our family.

Thank you for believing in me, even when I struggled to believe in myself.

Thank you for your countless sacrifices that often went unnoticed.

I want you to know how proud I am of you.

You are compassionate.

You are passionate.

You are generous.

You are loving.

You are resilient.

You are intelligent.

Most of all, you are a woman after God's own heart.

Never doubt that God sees every sacrifice you've made.

He has seen every tear you've cried.

He has heard every prayer you've whispered.

He has not forgotten you.

Sometimes, those who spend their lives pouring into others wonder when it will be their turn.

My daughter, your season is coming.

Hold on to God's unchanging hand.

Continue trusting Him, even when you cannot see what He is doing.

His timing is perfect.

The seeds you have planted in faith, obedience, love, and sacrifice will produce a harvest in God's appointed time.

Better days are not just coming…

They are already being prepared for you by the One who loves you most.

Never stop believing.

Never stop praying.

Never stop trusting.

The same God who carried you this far will faithfully lead you into everything He has promised.

I honor you.

I celebrate you.

I thank God for you.

And I love you more than words could ever say.

With all my love,

Mom

"For I know the plans I have for you," declares the Lord, "plans to prosper you and not to harm you, plans to give you hope and a future."
– Jeremiah 29:11

Dedication to My Bestie

To My Best Friend, Pastor Cynthia Johnson,

Thank you for accepting me and loving me through the good, the bad, and the ugly.

You've seen me at my strongest and at my weakest, yet you never walked away.

People often ask, *"Can anything good come out of Katrina?"*

Without hesitation, my answer is **YES!**

One of God's greatest blessings to me was bringing you into my life.

Thank you for pushing me when I wanted to quit.

Thank you for leading me when I needed direction.

Thank you for encouraging me when I doubted myself.

Thank you for listening without judgment.

But most of all…

Thank you for loving me unconditionally.

Your friendship has been a gift from God, and your faithfulness has reminded me what genuine sisterhood looks like.

You have celebrated my victories, prayed with me through my struggles, wiped away my tears, and continually pointed me back to God.

You are truly **the MVP** in my life.

I thank God for our friendship, our ministry, our laughter, and the purpose He has joined us together to fulfill.

Our team isn't just surviving…

Our team is WINNING!

I love you, Sis, and I pray God's richest blessings continue to overflow in your life.

Thank you for being the sister God knew I needed.

With love always,

Me

About the Author

Dr. Tonja L. Alexander is a native of Peoria, Illinois, and now resides in Texas, where she continues to answer God's call to minister, mentor, and serve. She is the founder of **W.I.N.N.E.R.S. (Women In Need Nurturing Edification Revitalizing Souls)**, a ministry dedicated to restoring hope, healing, and purpose to women and children who have experienced domestic violence, abuse, trauma, and life-altering challenges.

An ordained pastor, evangelist, mentor, and compassionate leader, Pastor Tonja has faithfully served in numerous ministry roles, including Armor Bearer, Administrator, and Co-Pastor. Her passion is helping individuals discover their identity in Christ while equipping them to overcome brokenness through the transforming power of God's love.

Through W.I.N.N.E.R.S., Pastor Tonja advocates for abused women and children by helping connect them with safe environments, resources, mentoring, and support as they begin their journey toward healing and restoration. She is committed to creating pathways of hope for families seeking freedom from abuse and the opportunity to rebuild their lives with dignity and purpose.

Pastor Tonja also has a heart for mentoring troubled teens, encouraging young women, and strengthening families through biblical teaching, practical guidance, and authentic love.

A divorced mother of six children including two whom she lovingly adopted, she is the proud grandmother of ten grandchildren and one great-grandson. Her life is a testimony of God's redeeming grace, proving that no past is too broken for God to restore.

Through her writing, ministry, and personal testimony, Pastor Tonja inspires others to stop searching for love in all the wrong places and discover the unconditional love, healing, and purpose found only in their Heavenly Father.

"Your past may explain your pain, but it does not determine your purpose. God's love has the final word."

Romans 10:8-13

8 But what saith it? The word is nigh thee, even
in thy mouth, and in thy heart: that is, the word
of faith, which we preach;
9 That if thou shalt confess with thy mouth the
Lord Jesus, and shalt believe in thine heart that
God hath raised him from the dead, thou shalt be
saved.
10 For with the heart man believeth unto
righteousness; and with the mouth confession is
made unto salvation.
11 For the scripture saith, Whosoever believeth
on him shall not be ashamed.
12 For there is no difference between the Jew and
the Greek: for the same Lord over all is rich unto
all that call upon him.
13 For whosoever shall call upon the name of the
Lord shall be saved.

Lord Jesus, I believe in my heart and confess with my mouth that You are Lord. Save me, forgive me, and make me Yours. Amen.

www.ingramcontent.com/pod-product-compliance
Lightning Source LLC
LaVergne TN
LVHW040515210926
848480LV00005BA/1470
9798996287529